THE OOP

Simplifying Finance & Economics
Through Basketball

John F. McMichael

Copyright © 2018 John F. McMichael
All rights reserved.
ISBN-13: 978-1722916121

Dedication

I would like to dedicate this book to my late parents, Diane Carol Jones and Sgt. John Floyd McMichael. This project has been the manifestation of all the seeds that were planted long ago; you watered my dreams with your love, and now the world gets to watch it all blossom. Time is a funny thing, and we all wish we had more of it. And while I wish I had more time with you guys, what you left me with is enough to last two lifetimes. I love you mom and dad.

Acknowledgements

I would like to thank my village – all of the friends and family members who have been mainstays in my life. You all inspire, challenge, encourage, support and love me like no other. With you guys in my corner, I feel as if the stars are within reach. You are my source of strength and energy. I love you all. I would also like to thank the game of basketball, and all of the coaches I've had along the way. This game has helped me make sense of life at times when nothing else really made sense. Finally, I would like to thank my soon-to-be wife, Ife Cooper-White. You continue to be one of my biggest fans, and I could not ask for a better life partner. We drive each other crazy sometimes, but I would not want to be crazy in love with anyone else. I love and appreciate every fiber of your being.

Introduction

There is a need for financial literacy. That much is apparent. However, what is not apparent is the methodology that should be used in order to convey the most important concepts in finance and economics. Further, what also becomes an obstacle is connecting the key terms and concepts to the audiences that need them the most.

More than anything, my aim is to present information that is easily understandable based on cultural congruence and practicality. Cultural congruence refers to communicating shared experiences through different mediums; it could be music, art, or fashion, but in this case, it's sports. In other words, I will speak your language when explaining the most pertinent aspects of financial literacy, and I will use your everyday activities to bring those ideas home.

One of the biggest hurdles to clear in any new environment is understanding jargon. Whether you move to a new neighborhood and the kids there have their unique lingo, or you're joining a new team that has its own special terms for basic plays, there's an adjustment period that you will have to overcome. It's very similar to the first time you picked up that pro playbook and your eyes glazed over.

Think of this as your playbook for understanding the once convoluted world of finance and economics. I will break down the barriers to entry and essentially lob you the easy "oop" so you can finish at the rim. The rim is the bank in this context!

Do you hear that, hoopers? I'm talking to y'all.

We've heard the horror stories, and we've seen the manifestation of poor financial decision making in documentaries like ESPN's, "Broke." A few things remain constant when examining why pro basketball players end up broke, and they're fairly simple and avoidable. Many players lack understanding, exposure, and discipline, all shortcomings that can be remedied using the same concepts that helped them get to the league in the first place.

While I refer to pro basketball players as the main topic of this text, the concepts will be applicable to everyday individuals who also want to learn. From the casual sports fan to the seasoned vet, you will be able to relate. Very similar to the game of basketball itself, it does not matter where you come from or how you appear to others; what matters most is a willingness to learn and work hard. While we explore this journey through the scope of the pro basketball player, be sure to utilize the base concepts to connect them to your "game" and life overall. Ten of the most important concepts that pro athletes need to understand are:

1. Scarcity

2. Supply and Demand

3. Cost-Benefit Analysis

4. Risk Tolerance

5. Asset Allocation

6. Net Worth

7. Liquidity

8. Time Value of Money & Compound Interest*

9. Inflation

*There are 9 chapters that include 10 total concepts. Chapter 8 combines two concepts: Time Value of Money & Compound Interest

Chapter 1: Scarcity

Positionless basketball and the Westbrook triple-double

What is **scarcity**? Do me a favor, sir, and walk over to the mirror. What do you see? Based on the fact that you don an NBA jersey with your name on the back, I can tell you a few things about yourself without ever meeting you. You're probably somewhere between the height of 6'6" and 6'8", and you're anywhere from 185 pounds to 230 pounds. (And for all of the "little guys" in the league who fall below those measurements, you are even more of a rarity).

You're also more mobile and coordinated than most everyday people. You can run fast, jump high, and dribble a basketball with ease. You've essentially secured 1 out of 491 job slots that millions of people hope and dream for. What I just laid out is exactly why you're **scarce**.

In other words, we can't just walk down any street or go into any gym and find someone with your combination of physical attributes and talent. In fact, there are over

7.5 billion people on Planet Earth, but less than 500 of those people end up on an NBA roster each year. That means you represent 0.0000007% of the population.

The shortage of any given entity describes the idea of scarcity. (1) Think about this: there are more billionaires than there are players in the NBA. Actually, there are more than 4.5 times as many billionaires in the world than there are players in the NBA at this very moment. (2) You, my friend, are the epitome of scarcity.

Why is scarcity an important concept and how does it work? Think about the latest pair of Jordan's, or that limited-edition Bugatti you saw. Now ask yourself about the prices. **The price or value rises when any given entity exists in small quantity.** Remember that you represent 0.0000007% of the population. You truly are a rare creature. Therefore, you are valuable! Know your worth and understand your position of power.

To take it a step further, take a look at the current landscape of the league. Once upon a time, a dominant, big man, who stood 7+ feet tall and could dominate the paint, was the most sought-after player. How do you think guys like Kwame Brown or Darko Milicic were top draft picks? You don't have to answer that.

However, because of market forces (the changing landscape of the league and the game becoming more marketable to a broader audience) we started seeing the need for more versatile players. Positionless basketball, which focuses on the interchangeability of players, has taken the NBA by storm. Why? Because the game has sped up, space is at a premium, and outside shooting is a must. On the other side of the ball, versatile players can switch defensively and guard multiple positions.

Now ask yourself, how many of those players exist in the NBA today? Those players usually occupy the upper echelon of the league ranks and are perennial all-stars/superstars. Thus, they're compensated (for the most part) for their rare feats and scarcity. **In sum, scarcity represents the absence of abundance.**

To bring this idea home, let's look at Russell Westbrook, aka the walking triple-double. Westbrook's rare combination of size, athleticism, ferocity, and skill allows him to affect every facet of the game. That could not have been more apparent than in the 2016-2017 NBA season, when he averaged a triple-double. He was then rewarded with three key things: league MVP, a hefty contract extension, and a place in the history books as only one of two players to EVER average a triple-double over an entire NBA season.

If something has only happened twice in the rich 68-year history of the NBA, that occurrence is scarce. (3) It follows that the individuals who accomplished this feat are scarce.

Therefore, their value, in our minds and relative to compensation, will reflect their scarcity; they are the players making the super-max! Since we cannot walk into any gym in America or abroad and find another Westbrook, he is a scarce or rare individual who we have to value appropriately. It's why he makes the big bucks, has multiple endorsements, is mentioned amongst the league's best, and is also considered one of the rarest point guards, if not athletes, to ever play basketball. Russell Westbrook = Scarcity!

At the time of this publication, Russell Westbrook ended the 2017- 2018 season averaging a triple-double, making him the first to ever average a triple-double in consecutive seasons.

Chapter 2:

Supply and Demand

MAKING YOUR MIDDLE SCHOOL TEAM & THE MIKE CONLEY EFFECT

The concept of **supply and demand** goes hand in hand with the concept of scarcity. Supply is simply the existence of a given entity, good, or service. Demand is the desire to acquire said entity, good, or service. (4) Remember your first basketball tryout? Think about how many young, eager faces lined up in that dimly-lit gym on that narrow baseline. Think about those wind sprints, defensive slides, layup lines, free throw shooting contests, scrimmages, etc.

Now forget all of that! What you should focus on is the personnel of the team you were trying to make. What were the **market forces/dynamics?** Were there already a bunch of upperclassmen on the squad? Were there a bunch of guards on the roster? Did they need a big man who could defend and grab rebounds? *The answers to those questions will go a lot further in explaining supply and demand.*

Let's say this was your middle school basketball team, and the universe of players was all of the kids between 6th and

8th grade. That reflects supply. Now, demand stems from the answers to those questions asked above. If the team is stacked with big men, guards will be in greater demand. Or if the team needs a lockdown wing defender, a premium (a higher price tag) will be placed on the boys who fit that mold. The premium placed on a good or service (or in this case, a player) directly relates to what the market deems as valuable.

So, if we're using the example of there being a bunch of big men on the team already, the demand for players who fit that position will be much lower than, say, guards. The *scarcity* of open positions on this team paired with an *oversupply* of big men, leads to a greater demand for guards. Therefore, there will be a higher demand for guards, and a lower demand for big men. That means that guards will be seen as more valuable and more likely to be picked for the team than big men. This is very similar to the process that occurs at the pro level. The most common place these decisions show up is during NBA free agency.

The most important thing to understand before truly delving into the nitty gritty of free agency and contract negotiations is *market dynamics*. In other words, what is the landscape of the league, and what kinds of guys will be the most sought after? When you approach free agency in this manner, not only do you have to assess supply and demand dynamics, but also you (or your agent) have to develop the appropriate strategy to maximize your potential earnings.

Think of it just like reading the defense. You survey the court (market), and you realize that the defense is making a concerted effort to clog the paint. Do you and your teammates continually drive into the teeth of the defense and hoist ill-advised shots over a defense that's both set and expecting the drive? Or do you use the drive to set up open jump shots for your shooters? The parallel here is knowing what to expect, and then adjusting your strategy accordingly. Therefore, if you are a deadeye shooter, it would behoove you to target the teams in the NBA who shoot terribly from the three because they will value you more (pay you more money), especially if there aren't many other deadeye shooters available on the market.

It also makes sense to know what the last free agent, deadeye shooter was paid (relative value), and what his impact was. Relative value gives you a reference point of where to start. For example, if the going rate for a knockdown shooter last year was $10 million a year and you're just as good or better, you would start your negotiations there. Similarly, when you're representing your talents to decision makers, focus on the parts of your game that make you marketable/desirable. Increase your demand!

When supply is limited, the demand for your skills increases, and therefore your price tag goes up.

Another interesting wrinkle that highlights the importance of understanding **market dynamics** is identifying the key factors that affect your market. For example, when you are a free agent looking to cash in on all the hard work you put into your craft, you should be aware of general business sentiment before you sign your contract. If we take a look at the 2016 NBA free agency, we can identify the factors that led to some of the more memorable contracts in sports. One player that immediately comes to mind is Mike Conley. Mike Conley has an excellent skill set for the point guard position (leadership, toughness, reliability, low maintenance). In many circles, Mike Conley would be considered severely underrated. However, the contract that he signed in 2016 shocked a lot of people. He signed a five- year, $153 million contract, which was the richest in NBA history at the time. (5) That's quite the price tag for someone who isn't considered in the upper echelon of NBA players, let alone elite players at his position. Mike Conley was the beneficiary of ripe market conditions. (These ripe market conditions extended to the overall economic market too, as businesses continued to post record profits.) Two things drove the payday that Mike Conley received: the NBA signed a new, lucrative TV deal that caused the salary cap to rise, and secondly, there weren't any elite, unrestricted point guards entering free agency. Therefore, business sentiment (TV deal, rising salary cap, higher team profits) led to teams feeling more incentivized to pay the big dollars. Mike Conley, while a very good basketball player, pretty much became a free agent at the perfect time.

(KD also became a free agent at a perfect time because the rise in the salary cap, along with Steph Curry still being on a very team-friendly contract, allowed the Warriors to sign a once-in-a-lifetime talent they wouldn't have been able to afford otherwise without completely reshaping their roster.)

What Mike Conley benefited from is similar to a big fish in a small pond. Mike Conley was essentially the young, decent looking guy who volunteered at the elderly home, and all the elderly women treated him like a heartthrob because his only competition was 87-year-old Mr. Hank.

Chapter 3:

Cost-Benefit-Analysis

HOW DO YOU SPEND YOUR TIME

IMPROVING YOUR GAME?

A **cost-benefit analysis** is exactly how it sounds: what will it cost me to undertake an endeavor, and how will its undertaking benefit me? (6) In other words, as a basketball player, is it more valuable to spend time shooting free throws or practicing ball handling? The answer to this question depends on various factors, but the most important factor will be how much work you will have to put in, and how much your game will benefit.

One thing that's important in basketball and in life is time. It's the one thing we cannot control; therefore, we must use it wisely. Back to the original example: we realize that ball handling and free throw shooting are both vital in the game of basketball. The question is, however, how should we prioritize either activity? We do a cost-benefit analysis. The way you approach this decision will rely upon a number of factors. What position do you play? How good/bad are you at either free throws or ball handling? How much time do you have? You get the picture.

If you're a point guard, ball handling will be more important to you than a center because point guards have the ball in their hands the most. Now if you have a "yo-yo" handle already, but you only shoot 75% from the free throw line, the decision is simple: you will benefit most by spending more TIME practicing free throw shooting. Therefore, if you have to designate a particular block of time to skill work, you would prioritize free throw shooting over ball handling because you won't see much added benefit to your handle, but you could certainly become a better free throw shooter; you may be able to go from 75% to 80% spending more time on practicing free throws.

Let's use a basic example of a normal day for player X. After player X handles all of his responsibilities and accounts for eating and sleeping, he has three to six hours to devote to working on his game. Three of those hours will automatically be dedicated to weightlifting, cardio, and film study as mandated by the team's staff. So, the remaining three hours or less will have to fit everything else. Player X divides his time equally into 30-minute blocks between mid-range shooting, long-range shooting, and live, in-game situations. Now he has a maximum of 1.5 hours left that he can spend on free throws and ball handling. Since player X has played point guard his entire life, he has elite handles. However, he loves honing his craft and would rather spend most of his time coming up with new dribble combinations to free up his overall floor game. The kicker is he's already an 83% free throw shooter, which is also very good. After realizing how much time he has left before he has to head home for dinner, player X concludes that spending more time shooting free throws can have a greater impact on his game. He comes to this conclusion because not only does he have more room to grow in this area, but also, he gets fouled a lot and is a league leader in trips to the charity stripe. Another factor impacting this decision is that player X is universally known as one of the best ball handlers in the league, so, in essence, he can't get much better in that area. It costs player X about 30 minutes more of free throw shooting than ball handling, but the overall impact of this decision has a greater effect on his individual game. This decision similarly impacts player X's team because adding a few percentage points onto your individual free throw shooting means more points for your team, and more points mean more team wins.

What we're seeing here is the fact that hoopers perform cost-benefit analyses every time they wake up, and even more so when they step into the gym. Just like in business when you have to assess an investment opportunity based upon the cost and potential return, basketball players have to assess how to best maximize their time in order to improve their overall game.

What I've described above is how players inherently make calculated decisions based on some very basic yet important economic principles. Underneath this larger analysis, there were other, smaller decisions happening simultaneously.

The recognition that spending more time on a skill that you've already perfected won't add much benefit is called the **law of diminishing marginal returns**. In other words, there comes a point where the benefit stops, and every minute spent beyond that point takes away from the overall benefit. (7)

In the example above regarding free throw shooting versus ball handling, we saw this play out pretty clearly. This is also evident in the weight room. When you're doing those single-leg deadlifts, there is a max amount of total reps (say 50) where anything above that begins to have the opposite effect. Instead of strengthening your balance and hamstrings, you begin to strain and compromise the very things you're trying to improve.

Another unique concept that was at play in the scenario laid out previously is every minute you spend practicing ball handling is a minute you're not spending shooting free throws; that's called a **trade-off**. Trade-offs then create **opportunity costs**. An opportunity cost is losing out on the benefit of one thing because you chose something else. (8)(9) The opportunity cost in this example is the idea that the choice you made to practice free throws removes the potential benefit you could have received from practicing ball handling.

Chapter 4:

Risk Tolerance

Shot selection & Steph's Shots

Oftentimes, when you hear **risk tolerance**, it is coming from a financial advisor, and he's probably pitching you some sort of investment idea. Risk tolerance is another term that is fairly straightforward and simple to comprehend. **In finance, risk tolerance refers to the level of risk you are comfortable with.** (10) A general, hard-and-fast rule is the younger you are, the more risk you are willing to take. The idea here is since you're young and curious, you are willing to take bigger risks, and ultimately if you do fail, you have a lot longer to bounce back. The opposite is usually true regarding older individuals who are usually conservative investors and will look to preserve their capital. To take a basic example, let's examine the investment approach by two different individuals.

Person A is a single, 25-year-old who just started her first real job with medical benefits and a company 401k. Person A enjoys riding her motorcycle to work, playing soccer on weekends, and traveling any chance she can.

Person B is 55 years old, has been working at the same company for 30 years, is married with three children who will be attending college soon, and has a home in the suburbs. Person B wakes up at the same time every day, travels the same route to work, loves crossword puzzles, and cycles with friends on the weekend when he's not on duty chaperoning his children to various activities.

Clearly, both individuals are at completely different places in their lives with very different responsibilities. Therefore, when it's time to make an investment decision, each person has to consider different factors based on his/her current situation (social, financial, relationship). One major component of any investment decision is the risk associated with said investment. Most people know where they stand when it comes to taking risks in everyday life. People who tend to gamble (with money, or their lives for that matter) are people who will have a high-risk threshold (tolerance), and historically may have participated in activities that most people would stay away from. Other people, who tend to play it safe, usually stick to routines, don't step very far out of their comfort zones, and like to be in control. Investing deals with a lot of very basic factors that are rooted in the type of person you are and your overall preferences.

If we go back to person A versus person B, we can guess, if given a risky investment versus a safe investment, how each one would typically decide. For simplicity purposes, let's say the two investment opportunities are as follow:

- Investment A: Biomedical stock for a company that's been cutting edge and profitable over the last three years but has some questions regarding its leadership.

- Investment B: A 30-year Apple bond yielding little over 3% yearly until 2048.

Let's quickly define some of these basic terms and how they work. A **stock** represents ownership in a publicly traded company. (11) So, if you buy one share of Apple's stock, you own a piece of the company. You now have **equity**. *When you think stock, think equity or ownership.* (12) The one share represents a very small ownership percentage as Apple has over five billion total shares *outstanding (outstanding in this case means available for purchase or sell).* While Apple is a very well-known company, the risk associated with owning Apple's stock is that the price where you bought it can go lower. It essentially can go down to zero, and you lose all of your money. On the flip side, there is no limit to how high Apple's stock can go, so your upside is essentially unlimited. There are a lot more nuances in between, but this is basically how stocks work.

Bonds are opposite in their features versus stocks. While stocks equal equity, bonds equal debt. The way a bond works is like a loan with interest. It just depends on who loans the money out, and who asked for (issued) the loan. Let's say you buy a 30-year Apple bond for $1,000 and agree to an **interest rate** of 3.75%. *(An interest rate represents the cost of borrowing. So, it costs Apple 3.75% to borrow your money.)* What you did was enter into an agreement where you agree to loan Apple $1,000 for a 30-year period, and during that period, they will pay you interest. The payment could be quarterly (once every three months) or semi-annually (every six months or twice a year). For this example, we're using a semi-annual interest payment schedule. Now, with an agreed upon interest rate of 3.75%, you receive $37.50 every six months for 30 years, and at the end of the 30 years you get your $1,000 back. That's called having your *principal* (original $1,000) returned at *maturity* (the end of the loan term, which was 30 years in this example). The bond type explained above may sound familiar, but you're probably most familiar with personally paying the interest—think home loans, car loans, and student loans.

But with those types of loans, you are not being compensated; you're paying down that debt. (13) Now that you understand each investment type, who do you think chooses investment A or B? If you said the young woman would choose the stock, and the older gentleman would choose the bond, that would be a very sound guess. For the sake of this example, that makes the most sense.

With finance, business, or investing overall, there aren't any guaranteed outcomes, but there are ways to think about things and approach decisions that will put you in the best position to succeed. It's just like basketball. Although you have your base balanced, your eyes locked on the rim, your elbows in, and you hold your follow-through, it does not guarantee the shot will go in. However, it will give you a really good chance of making that shot.

This leads me to the biggest parallel between risk tolerance and shot selection. The types of shots you take during a game say a lot about you as a player, the same way that the types of investment decisions you make say a lot about you as a person. If you take good, efficient shots, you are probably a disciplined player. If you take wild, ill-advised shots, you are probably an erratic, undisciplined player.

Approach the types of shots you take in a game just like you approach risk. The higher the degree of difficulty or risk, the more likely you are to miss. You know those guys who take long, contested two-pointers with 20 seconds to go on the shot clock! How about the guy who drives to the basket where there are two seven-footers waiting, and instead of going straight up, he makes it more difficult by double and triple clutching. All the coach can do on the sideline is shake his head and call a sub; just like your investment adviser would shake his head at the prospect of you buying a beach house in Idaho.

That said, risk is not a bad thing when managed well. One way to manage risk is to make sure your moves are calculated. Let's take Steph Curry for a moment, the king of the great, bad shot!

If you watch Steph Curry play, you probably have noticed his video-game like handle, and his otherworldly jump shot, both from a standstill and off the dribble. His form is exquisite, his fundamentals are impeccable, and he is hands down the best overall shooter in NBA history! (I personally think Klay is a better spot-up shooter). If you REALLY watch Steph play, you will notice that based on what is widely accepted as a good shot, a lot of Steph's shots would traditionally be considered bad shots. However, and this is lost on a lot of young kids playing the game, Steph Curry practices those same shots for hours and hours. Every shot Steph has taken in the game, he has taken that same shot thousands of times in practice. Fans only get to see a glimpse of Steph's hard work during his pre-game dribbling routine or his pre-game court work. The shots that Steph takes would make most coaches shudder in disgust as evidenced by his coach Steve Kerr's face on one of the more memorable basketball sequences over the past couple seasons. Steph Curry uses a screen from Andrew Bogut going left, he puts together a between-the-legs-behind-the- back combo while being surrounded by FOUR defenders (one of whom is Chris Paul), seems to momentarily lose his way, only to find himself going away from the basket while being tracked by TWO defenders now; Steph takes one hard dribble farther away from the basket where he looks as if he's trying to escape the defenders, and suddenly, BANG! He turns on the drop of a dime, barely squares his shoulders, and hoists a 25-foot, three-pointer over the two trailing defenders. To make this crazier, there were nine seconds left on the shot clock! The most important thing to watch during this play is Steve Kerr's outstretched arms and puzzled look as if to say, "Why would you take that shot?," which immediately turns into a head palm after

Steph nails the shot.

I've painted this picture for two specific reasons. The first is to show that shot selection and risk, for that matter, are relative. It's relative to the person taking that shot or risk. Although his own coach was looking at Steph like he lost his mind, Steph knew exactly what he was doing because he practiced those moves and those shots so many times before.

The second, more important reason is to highlight that while some individuals make awe-inspiring plays that look effortless, there is a lot of work that goes into pulling off amazing feats. What a lot of younger players or new investors fail to realize is the process that goes into being great at a given task. It takes a ton of preparation.

Risk tolerance is most akin to shot selection because it shows how individuals are either bound by their limitations or emboldened by their hard work and ability. You wouldn't catch Deandre Jordan taking one-legged, off-balance three-pointers with 2 defenders draped to him because that is not a part of his arsenal. It's too big of a risk! Those aren't the shots he practices tirelessly. Those are "Steph Shots." It's the same idea that limits Steph from acting as the screener in a pick and roll and then diving to the rim to catch an alley-oop. It's too big of a risk! So, what may limit Steph physically, empowers DJ and vice versa. If we tie this back to business and assessing an individual's risk tolerance, we see that people are more or less comfortable with given decisions based on a myriad of reasons: personality, comfort, understanding, practice, etc.

Chapter 5:

Asset Allocation

THE LEBRON EFFECT!!!

Asset allocation describes how individuals balance risk versus reward. (14) If your mom was anything like mine, she probably told you, "Don't put all of your eggs in one basket." If that resonates, your mom was quite the oracle. The concept of spreading around your risk is one of the oldest, most effective investment strategies.

When you decide to spread around risk, you are diversifying. (15) It's very similar to being an all-around player in basketball. When you can only do one thing extremely well, it is very easy for your opponent to take it away. If you're a great shooter, and all you do is shoot jump shots, your game is predictable. Everyone knows what to expect, so you're much easier to defend. The same concept extends to finance and investing. If you hold all of your money in one given investment or asset, your overall financial health will be very limited. Your risk will be concentrated in one area, and if that particular investment or asset does not work out, you lose everything. The concept of asset allocation comes into play when building a portfolio. Think of a portfolio the same way you think of a given player's skill set. The best players in the league are usually multi-faceted, all-around players. Similarly, the best performing portfolios are those that are diversified. Let's take a look at the LeBron effect...

If you've had the pleasure of watching LeBron James play the game of basketball, one of the first things that jumps off the screen (or court if you've seen him play in person) is his utter physical dominance. LeBron is a once-in-a-lifetime physical specimen, and his athleticism occupies the upper echelon of every major sport EVER. On the surface alone, these attributes would be more than enough to give someone like LeBron a leg up on the competition; however, if you know basketball the way I do, those surface characteristics are not nearly enough to be a great player. The remarkable thing about LeBron is the fact that outside of his physical gifts, he is very adept at nearly every other aspect of the game of basketball. LeBron has a diverse skill set, potentially the most diverse skill set we've ever seen in the game. But what does that mean, and why is it relevant? What I'm getting at is what makes LeBron one of the greatest players ever.

In order to be a great basketball player, you have to master the game. That sounds simple enough, right? Well, mastering the game of basketball is a lot more involved and difficult than most people would think. Sure, some guys master shooting. Others master ball handling. A few guys master defense. A handful of guys master leadership. But putting all of those things together and reaching a level of mastery is like making the perfect gumbo. Just a pinch of this, a smidge of that, a little more of this and less of that, all of this and none of that. Sounds complicated, huh? That's because it is, but not for the reason you think. The game of basketball itself is very simple. But mastering the game of basketball is complicated.

Mastering the game of basketball does not mean mastering every aspect of the game; rather, it means finding the perfect balance between your physical gifts and your mental wits.

This concept is what makes LeBron one of the greatest ever. Think about it. He's not the tallest in the league. He's not the fastest in the league (see Westbrook and John Wall). He's not the best ball handler (see Kyrie Irving). He's not the best shooter (see Mr. Risk Tolerance himself, Steph Curry). He's not the best defender (see Draymond Green or a healthy Kawhi Leonard). You get the point. LeBron is unique because, although he may not be the best at any one thing, he is very good at many different things. What's even more impressive is he has the ability to be the best at any given thing *when he needs to be*.

Asset allocation is very much the same in that it means deploying the right amount of capital, at the right time, and in the right areas. When the market is going up, it may seem like a great idea to ride the wave by placing all of your money into stocks. Or since the game of basketball has become more focused on three-point shooting, it may seem like you should spend all of your time on perfecting your stroke from beyond the arc. However, just like we mentioned earlier, placing all of your emphasis (risk) in one area is never a good strategy. If the stock market corrects (it always does), you risk losing all of your money. If you had spread that risk around, for example, and bought stocks, bonds, real estate, art, etc., you would fare a lot better because of the very nature of certain investments; they do well when others do poorly.

Bonds generally perform well when stocks perform poorly, for example.

On the other hand, if you worked on your handle, a floater, your ability to get into the paint, and getting your teammates involved, it doesn't handicap you when someone continually chases you off the three-point line.

You have the ability to be a threat and perform well

because you have a diversified skill set. Your assets are allocated effectively. *Asset allocation is all about maximizing your returns, aka making the most of what you've got.*

Having all of the tools at your disposal, but not knowing when and how to use them is pointless. To connect this idea to everyday life, if you give a normal person $50 million dollars tomorrow, they'd probably run out of money in a matter of a few years (if that). There are estimates out there that say more than 70% of lotto winners end up broke within three to five years. (16)

Do you see the parallel to pro basketball players? Why do people who are so fortunate to receive large amounts of money end up broke? It is because they lack understanding, exposure, and discipline. If you lack understanding, you cannot make informed decisions. If you've never been exposed to a given experience, you do not know how to navigate it. And lastly, if you do not have discipline to enact what you've learned or to stick to a given plan, you will set yourself up for failure.

The reason why LeBron is so special is because he has maximized not only his physical gifts and talents, but also his focus on the most important part of the game of basketball: the mental aspect. It has been said that LeBron has a savant-like memory and can recall opponent's plays from years prior. Oftentimes, LeBron is playing the game three or four steps ahead of everyone else, and that can be evidenced by his ability to, almost like a QB in football, "throw guys open." In other words, LeBron, who plays small forward, passes the ball to places on the court where players ideally are supposed to be in order get the best shot; this is a skill reserved for the league's best point guards. On any given night, you may see LeBron guarding three to four positions, running the offense, or putting the ball in the basket himself from everywhere on the court. LeBron's physical dimensions certainly help the cause, but it's what's between his ears that truly propels him towards greatness. Mr. James understands not only the nuances of the game of basketball, but also how to prepare his mind and body to continually perform at an optimal level. In year 15, it is evident that LeBron places a premium on his training, health, and nutrition, so much so that he is actively challenging how we view longevity. It can be argued that no one in the history of the NBA (or even sports) has benefitted from peak performance for as long as LeBron has.

LeBron's prowess also extends well beyond the hardwood as evidenced by his business success, philanthropic generosity, and, more recently, his vocal civic engagement. LeBron does not need to play another minute of basketball, and at the tender age of 33, he has secured the futures of generations to come. He also has made savvy investments away from sports that will keep him busy and productive well into his twilight years. LeBron James has fully embraced his duty as a role-model, and continually inspires people, who would normally be forgotten about, "to strive for greatness."

Where LeBron sits on the pantheon of success at this very moment epitomizes the idea of asset allocation. *His life is diversified!!!* Remember, asset allocation is how you balance risk, and the best way to balance risk is to diversify.

The parallel in basketball is how players diversify their skill sets in order to be most effective. Having the right balance of skill and IQ allows players to maximize their return!

LeBron has taken that to a whole new level. He is redefining how we view athletes by doing what most people in sports and everyday life fail to do: he is taking full advantage of all of his opportunities and fulfilling his greatest potential. LeBron James could have easily headlined any number of previous chapters, which a true testament to just how multi-layered he is.

Chapter 6: Net Worth

THE REAL PLUS MINUS

Net worth is all of your assets minus all of your liabilities. **Assets** can be precious metals (silver, gold, platinum), cash, a house, art, businesses, etc. **Liabilities** are debt. **Debt** is money you owe to either an individual or entity. (17) A few examples of the most common types of debt are credit card balances, home loans, automobile loans, and student loans. In other words, your net worth is what you get you when you take everything you own that has value and measure it against everything you owe. The result will either be negative or positive. Therefore, you want your assets to be greater than your liabilities.

Your net worth is very much like your plus/minus in basketball because it measures your overall effect on the game, and whether or not it is negative or positive. Assets are like strengths in basketball. Think of assets like having a handle, a silky jump shot, crazy athleticism, a high IQ, and a non-stop motor. Liabilities are weakness on the court like turnovers, horrible defense, bad attitude, and selfishness.

Some players have very valuable assets but can also hurt their team because their liabilities outweigh their assets. We have all seen a player who has an amazing offensive arsenal, but gets glued to the bench because he can't pass, does not play defense, and he has a poor attitude. Having notable assets doesn't always mean that your overall game is net positive. This concept extends to your net worth as well.

If I have $1 million in cash (between checking, savings, and retirement accounts), $50,000 in jewelry, a $2 million home, and three Bentleys, but I owe the bank $10 million for various credit card balances and car/home loans, I am essentially broke. My net worth is NEGATIVE. I owe more money than I currently have. The keyword in the previous sentence was "currently."

The gift and the curse for most professional basketball players is that their prime earning years happen much earlier than the rest of the population. Pro basketball players earn millions of dollars when they're in their late teens and early twenties, while most adults won't earn their largest paychecks until they're well into their forties. The gift is those guys earn huge salaries, but the curse is with youth comes lack of experience. It's quite the conundrum; you earn most of your money when you know the least!

That's one of the main goals of this book: to provide younger professional basketball players exposure to the world of finance and economics, so they can be better prepared to excel on and off the court. Similarly, just as I mentioned in the very first paragraph, these concepts are for everyday individuals as well, so be sure to apply them to your unique situation.

The key takeaway when examining net worth is that you want your net worth to be POSITIVE. It's great to have assets and all that comes along with them.

However, what's even better is to have those assets far outweigh your liabilities. When people or even companies have more liabilities than they do assets, it's only a matter of time before their financial health becomes strained.

It's similar to dieting and exercise. If you exercise regularly, but you eat poorly and don't properly hydrate, your body will eventually suffer. Your muscles may look cool in a t-shirt, but your insides are compromised. This thinking extends to the court too. We live in a time where highlights are prioritized, and stats are king. We crave instant gratification, and that extends to our professional basketball players too. We want to "ooh" and "aah" when a player hits a deep three or dunks it over two people. Also, we love to see those gaudy stat lines. Over the past few seasons, we've become enamored with the triple–double, not so much for its rarity, but rather for its cachet. When a player puts up 35 points, 15 rebounds, and 12 assists, no one asks what that player's plus/minus was. Most people won't even ask what the outcome of the game was.

However, those are extremely vital questions. If that same player was a net negative to his team and they lost, does that triple-double really matter? What if that player had 12 turnovers, shot 40% from the field on 30 shots, missed eight free throws, and the guy he was guarding had an efficient 42 points, eight rebounds, eight assists, no turnovers, and only took 15 shots? How would you view that original stat line then?

Remember our example from earlier. You can have all the nice assets like money, cars, and jewelry, but if your liabilities far outweigh those assets, you're broke! The lesson here is while perception may seem like reality, the true measure of worth is a bit more layered than surface objects. We should aspire to have overwhelmingly positive net worth, just like ball players should aspire to have overwhelmingly positive impacts on the game. That's the true measure of worth. After all is said and done, what do I have left? That's your net worth. Once the last buzzer sounds, were you a net negative or net positive to your team? That's your plus/minus.

Chapter 7: Liquidity

"Dame Time" … "Practice??? We talkin' bout practice???"

For simplicity purposes, think of liquidity as the measure of how quickly you can turn an asset into cash. (18) You've heard the saying, "Cash is King." That is because it has universal value and can be used as a medium of exchange. Remember when we spoke about net worth? Net worth is about how much you truly have, while *liquidity* measures how fast you can prove it. In other words, you can be worth $5 million on paper, but a large portion of that $5 million could potentially be tied up in stocks, bonds, real estate, art, etc.

Liquidity is important for various reasons, but one of the most important reasons is liquidity essentially allows you to always be prepared for the unexpected. In an emergency, like a medical event or a death in the family, or even an investment opportunity, being able to produce cash to either cover the cost or take advantage of an opportunity is crucial. Being liquid allows you to play offense and defense! From a defensive standpoint, you can always be prepared for "Armageddon," or be well equipped to deal with an emergency. Offensively, you can go after opportunities that arise quickly, or take advantage of the perks that come with having cash (think discounts or favorable terms).

Liquidity is relative as well. Cash is the most liquid, and we've used that for our overarching examples thus far. However, a check is also liquid, as long as the person writing it has the cash in the bank to fund it. Certain stocks, ones that are actively traded by a large number of people, are also liquid. You know that if and when you need to convert your stock to cash, there will be someone willing to pay a given price for it. That price, as we discussed earlier, will be contingent upon supply and demand dynamics.
Other stocks that don't trade very frequently are a lot less liquid or what we call **illiquid.** Illiquid means that your ability to turn the assets that you own into cash is sorely lacking.

For example, if all of your cash in tied up in real estate (we know not to do that though because we understand asset allocation), it will be very difficult to sell your place very quickly and pull the cash out. Sometimes it could take months or years to sell real estate, not to mention market dynamics could potentially hinder you from selling at a price that you think is optimal. The levels of liquidity vary based upon the asset, as you can see. **The faster you can turn an asset into cash, the more liquid it is.**

Quick note: In no world would I ever tell you to hoard cash because you will learn later that cold, hard cash doesn't benefit from the magic of compound interest. That said, there are events in life that require immediacy, and being liquid certainly makes things much easier.

Let's bring the idea of liquidity to life with an examination of two players who exhibit the liquidity characteristics on the floor, but in different ways: Damian Lillard and Allen

Iverson. Mr. Dame Time himself, and Mr. Practice??? himself.

When the stakes are the highest and the clock ticks towards zero, one of the few guys who remain calm while others panic is Damian Lillard. The part of the game that I'm describing above is crunch time, aka where the greats separate themselves. Therefore, it must be noted that Damian Lillard, in essence, has had crunch time renamed to "Dame Time." You know it when you see it. The game is tight. The pace is frenetic. Every possession feels like the last. Guys are exhausted. Coaches are stressed. Everything about this moment screams intensity, yet there is one guy who calmly surveys the scene, looks down at his wrist as if he's checking his watch, pats said wrist, and proclaims, "You know what time it is." Yup, it's Dame Time! Damian Lillard has hit his fair share of game winners and clutch shots during his young career. What's most impressive is Dame's stoic demeanor and seemingly unflappable game.

Damian Lillard's game is liquid. In the most tense, emergency-like moments, he remains calm and executes time and time again.

In life or in business, when an unexpected expense arises, how will you handle it? Will you be cool, calm, and collected? You would be if you knew you had the cash to cover said expense the same way Damian Lillard knows he has the game to flourish in the clutch! Being liquid bails you out of emergency situations the same way a clutch player bails his team out of really tight games because you know if all fails, you have the big Joker. However, liquidity isn't only useful for emergency situations. Let's take a look at Allen Iverson, aka A.I., aka The Answer, aka Mr. Practice.

Almost 16 years ago, a frustrated and upset Allen Iverson uttered the word practice 22 times in one press conference. It has become a meme for the ages, and even casual basketball fans immediately think of that famous moment whenever they hear someone say practice. What's really interesting about this backdrop is what makes Allen Iverson so special. Painted as the man who scoffed at the idea of practice, Allen Iverson gave his blood, sweat, and tears every time he stepped onto the court. That's important because for someone who was rumored to have questionable practice and training habits, Allen Iverson could give you 40 points in his sleep AND will his team to victories; all 6-foot, 165 pounds of him.

This is the epitome of liquidity. How fast and easily can you turn an asset into cash? In Allen Iverson's case, how fast and easily can he turn his talents into buckets and wins? The answer is immediately. (See what I did there?) Whether or not Allen Iverson practiced or spent hours in the gym didn't matter much once he stepped onto the court because he literally could electrify a crowd and galvanize a group of men. Allen Iverson is what we call in the basketball world, "a walking bucket," which means anytime he touches the ball, it's an almost certainty that he will score. And in a game where your team wins if it scores more than the opposition, being able to manufacture buckets is critical.

Allen Iverson's game is akin to being able to take advantage of a great investment opportunity that is time sensitive. Imagine you've had your eye on an investment property for years because it was fairly priced, in a great neighborhood, and you knew the owner, Ms. Linda, would sell after she retired at year's end. However, instead of retiring at the end of the year, Ms. Linda's company gave her garden leave. Therefore, instead of retiring to Florida in December, Ms. Linda wanted to sell her house immediately and make arrangements to move down to Boca. Being the nice lady she is, she gives you a call and lets you know the good news: she gets her full retirement a few months early, and now the house you've been coveting is on the market.

What is the first thing that goes through your mind? It's probably, "Wow, that's much sooner than I expected. How fast can I get the funds to lock down this property before it hits the open market?" If you're liquid, this is welcomed news, and you're excited. It's not a mad dash or scramble in order to raise the funds. You're in a prime position to go on the offensive and take full advantage of a great opportunity. You tell Ms. Linda that not only will you buy at asking price, but you will buy the house all in cash as soon as you both get all the administrative work done. Both parties are happy because Ms. Linda gets to live full time in her Florida home months earlier than initially expected, and with a nice chunk of cash to help with her transition. And you're happy because you know you've bought a great property that you researched for years at a great price. The fact that you were liquid eliminated the stress of having to come up with the funds, on one hand, and also eliminated a potential bidding war in the event that Ms. Linda put the property on the open market.

To summarize, liquidity measures how quickly you turn an asset into cash. Liquidity comes into play in emergency situations like clutch moments in basketball—Dame Time. Similarly, liquidity allows you to take advantage of opportunities immediately when they're presented, just like Allen Iverson being able to drop 40 points without having to… you've guessed it: practice.

Chapter 8:

Time Value of Money and Compound Interest

THE VALUE OF YOUNG TALENT!!!

Time value of money is one of the most interesting concepts in finance. Have you ever heard the saying, "a bird in hand is worth two in the bush?" It means having something tangible right now is more valuable than the prospect of potentially getting something greater in the future. In finance, one dollar today is not worth the same one dollar in the future. (19) Most people understand the idea of inflation, but we'll get to that later. The reason why one dollar today is not worth one dollar in the future is because you can invest that dollar today and reap the benefits of compound interest. **Compound interest** is when your money makes money! (20) Simple enough, right?

Referring back to the bird in the bush idiom, it's a smarter play to have something now that you can grow rather than get the same measly $1 20 years from now. Remember when we discussed liquidity, and I said I would never tell you to hoard cash? The reasoning is displayed beautifully by examining the concept of time value of money and compound interest. Let's go through an example that drives this idea home.

Two brothers, Skeptical and Savvy, receive a lump sum of cash after suing an amusement park for being injured on one of their rides. They were each awarded $1 million. Skeptical, after receiving his share, immediately puts all of his money in a safe. Savvy, on the other hand, calls up his local bank and inquires about setting up a savings account. Savvy tries to get his brother to do the same, but being the pessimist that he is, Skeptical decides to keep his money "under his mattress" because he doesn't trust banks. He even challenges his brother Savvy by saying, "I don't know how you can put all your money into an account and expect it to still be there. Let's make a bet that I'll do things my way and you do things your way, and in 20 years, I bet I have more money than you in my safe. The only rule is you cannot add any outside money to your account, and I cannot add any outside money to my safe." They agree.

While Skeptical didn't trust banks, what he should have trusted was compound interest.

Over the next 20 years, Skeptical banks on the fact that his brother is not only taking a big risk putting all of his money in the bank, but also that he will spend some. Skeptical literally doesn't touch any of the $1 million for 20 years. He just knew that his brother would spend some of his. What he didn't know is that his brother did not touch any of his money either, and the savings account that he set up was an interest-bearing account. The account gained 5% interest and was compounded annually. Here's what that means and why compound interest is magic. At the end of year one, Savvy earned 5% on his $1 million dollars for a total balance of $1,050,000. He earned $50,000 by doing nothing. His money worked while he slept. It gets even better… So next year, guess what happens? He gets 5% again. BUT, he gets 5% on $1,050,000, making his balance at the end of year two $1,102,500. Savvy made $102,000 in two years without raising a finger. Let's keep this going, so you can see just how magical compound interest is.

At the start of year three, Savvy has $1,102,500 in his account, but our magical friend compound interest comes along and pays him 5%. He ends year three with $1,157,625, a whopping $157,625 gain in three years because Savvy woke up and brushed his teeth in the morning. You get the picture, right? **Compound interest is cool because your interest makes interest, or put another way, your rewards get rewarded.** So instead of just receiving 5% every year based on your $1 million starting point, you get rewarded by getting 5% of your new profits without ever making any adjustments or additions. This is what it means when someone says, "Make your money work for you." What they're describing is compound interest.

Let's go back and visit Savvy and Skeptical. At the end of 20 years, how much does each brother have? Well, Skeptical's math is easy. He kept his money under his mattress and never spent or added any. Therefore, he has $1 million. Savvy, on the other hand, parked his money in an interest-bearing account where he was guaranteed 5% compounded annually. At the end of 20 years, Savvy's account balance is a whopping $2,653,297.71!!! Savvy nearly triples his money while Skeptical's money did absolutely nothing but collect dust. (For those of you who are math nerds, the equation to find how Savvy earned over $2 million is: $1,000,000*1.05^{20}$. The $1 million is the original principal, the 1.05 represents the 5% interest rate, and 20 represents the number of years.

The value of compound interest shows itself over the long haul, which is why investing has always been about the long game. This concept is shared in basketball front offices everywhere as it pertains to evaluating talent, especially young talent. Think about how many times you've heard franchises mention their *investment* in acquiring young talent via the NBA draft or free agency. The NBA draft is literally an event dedicated entirely to securing the types of young talent that could potentially change a franchise or even a city! It's the same idea when you're building a portfolio; you want to make the right investments early and allow them to grow and flourish, so one day in the future they will represent a great monetary return. When an organization evaluates young talent, they're mostly envisioning what that player will become.

There are only 60 jobs handed out every June as a part of the NBA draft, so franchises have to make very calculated decisions.

Teams have to understand their risk tolerance, asset allocation, costs versus benefits, and liquidity just the same way an investor has to when evaluating their portfolio. Every investment, whether in an asset or a player, comes along with inherent risk. If a team considers drafting a young, titillating talent who has already suffered a few injuries, they have to understand that there's risk associated with that player. They risk drafting the player too high and having the unfortunate occurrence of said player getting injured. On the other hand, if they pass on this player, they have to potentially contend with a competitor drafting him and that player going on to become an all-time great. Some general mangers' jobs are lost or secured based upon these decisions, especially as it pertains to evaluating young talent.

Asset allocation from a team perspective deals with understanding how drafting a certain young player will fit into the overall culture and chemistry of the team. If the team already has a dearth of young guards, bringing another young guard into that fold could be problematic. You could potentially have too many players or assets concentrated in one area. Remember, diversification is key, so you would be better off filling a need elsewhere on your team. Similarly, front offices have to decide what a player will cost versus how much they can benefit from his services. If a team has a player on their draft board at 10, but there are rumblings that the player may not last that long, a team can consider trading up. The question then becomes, what will it cost to move up in the draft, and what is the benefit associated with that decision?

Liquidity also comes into play when evaluating young talent or any talent for that matter. From a strictly dollars and cents standpoint, teams have a salary cap to contend with, and for the most part, they have to stick within those constraints; going over the salary caps comes with stiff penalties akin to overdrafting in your checking account. Remember when we spoke about liquidity being able to quickly prove how much you're worth? Teams face a similar dilemma in sports, specifically basketball.

For example, if a player becomes available in free agency, how can you take the requisite steps financially to secure that player's services if you're already at or above the salary cap? This is why some GMs make the big bucks; they have to move around salaries to make the math work, and moving around salaries is just like buying and selling stocks in a sense. If you want to sign player X, it will cost Y. But in order to secure player X's services, you need to trade (sell) player Z. How easily tradable (liquid) is player Z? If he's easily tradable, he (or technically his contract) is liquid, and you have a better chance of making the money work in order to sign your intended target.

As you can see, some of the most important concepts in finance/economics have multiple applications and can be portrayed in various ways. Once you know how to identify these concepts, you begin seeing them in your everyday life. One of the beautiful things about being human is we can connect ideas and concepts based on our shared experiences; this is what allows us to relate to each other and the world at large.

The picture I laid out here is the epitome of the time value of money represented through the concept of compound interest. The reason why a dollar today is not worth a dollar in the future is because you can invest that dollar today and earn compound interest. This idea extends beyond finance and can be clearly seen in the landscape of the current NBA.

You know what compound interest looks like from a player perspective? What do the following players have in common? Ben Simmons, Joel Embid, Karl Anthony Towns, Giannis Antetokounmpo, Kyrie Irving, Anthony Davis, Kristaps Porzingis, Bradley Beal, Devin Booker, and Nikola Jokic. Outside of Giannis, Devin, and Nikola, all of these guys were top five draft picks. What's more impressive is that, at the time of me writing this, every single player listed above is 25 or younger!!! Beyond that, each player listed is a franchise cornerstone and already some of the best at their given positions. So how exactly do they represent the time value of money and compound interest? First, a rookie contract today is not worth what it will be worth in the future. That's an easy concept to understand when it comes to the NBA because rookies, relative to their skill and seniority, are paid less than more established, veteran stars. However, as we mentioned previously, these guys were drafted so high because of their potential returns in the future. They will hone their talents, get faster, stronger, smarter, and as their game rounds out, they will become the established superstars of the league. And as they begin to occupy the upper echelon of the league, what was once a rookie contract, becomes a super- max deal worth north of $200 million. Now that's compound interest with a twist!

The reason why NBA players are so special is because they benefit from the same business/economic principles as everyday people; it's just a lot faster and a lot more lucrative. A rookie, in a matter of three or four years, can turn a $5-6-million-dollar salary to a $30-40-million-dollar salary. **If NBA players, once they've reached max status, realized that they've not only won the genetic lottery, but also the actual lottery to an extent, they would be more inclined to focus on protecting and growing their wealth.**

Protecting and growing your wealth first starts with making informed decisions. A wise man once said, "If you know better, you'll do better." What that means for athletes and everyday individuals is first stepping outside of your comfort zone. I know it sounds scary, but if you thought about your comfort zone like a perimeter around you, growth only begins right beyond that perimeter. If you're comfortable, you're not growing. The scariest part about finance, business, or economics for me was always the jargon. It always sounded so sophisticated and intimidating.

Then, when you add in numbers and graphs, it becomes like deciphering hieroglyphics. Trust me, I get it.

During the course of my young career, I've crunched so many numbers, looked at so many graphs, and made so many decisions based on all of that data; and the thing that I learned is that numbers or graphs or concepts mean nothing without context. Therefore, what I am trying to provide in this book is context. Earlier, I referred to it as cultural congruence because sports itself is a culture. Cultural congruence, represented in everyday life, is the proverbial head nod. Some of you immediately knew exactly what I was referring to. For those of you who are a little lost, bear with me.

Picture a sunny, summer afternoon in Bed-Stuy, Brooklyn. It's 1998, and I am on my way to the corner store. As I approach the store, there's a group of young, teenage boys. I don't recognize any of these guys, but over the years, you learn the tricks of the trade navigating NYC's streets. So I made eye contact with a few guys and gave them the "head nod." Not too long, not too short. Not a lot of eye contact, but just enough. The guys all nodded back as if they approved my passage to the corner store. This may seem dramatic, but the way I navigated that situation could have been the difference between a safe passage home and a not-so-safe passage home. Teenage boys with little to do in the summer find ways to get into mischief, and that mischief presents itself in many different forms. Some pull pranks, some joyride, and some rough up unsuspecting and unfamiliar 10-year-olds. I can write an entire book on the layers presented here, but what I learned then is what I keep with me today. It's part savvy, part street smarts, and part fearlessness that over the years has become polished poise.

The reason I told this story is because I wanted to accomplish two things: relate to those who experienced the same things and were able to head nod their way out. And for a second group of people who may not have experienced any of it but are open to learning from others' experiences and implementing the head nod into their lives. The head nod represents an unspoken understanding for many; for others, it says everything is all right and we're on the same team.

Here and now, we are on the same team of enlightenment and exposure. This book is intended to bring together the strangest of bedfellows, people from all walks of life who simply want better lives. We know how much being financially literate and responsible is a necessity in our world, and the good news is, we're not alone.
Empowerment is my aim, and information is my game. The more information I am able to gather and pass along, the better off we all are.

Chapter 9: Inflation

MY DOLLAR DOESN'T GO AS FAR AS IT ONCE DID... EMPTY STATS...

When I was a kid, I would run errands for my parents, elders on my block, and other family members. Some errands included going to the corner store (or as some of my fellow New Yorkers call it, the bodega), the grocery store, a local restaurant, the post office, etc. For taking a couple minutes out of my busy day, I would be compensated $1. The absolute best was when my mom allowed me to keep the change for running one of the aforementioned errands. I became adept at getting everything on the errand list for a few dollars cheaper than my mom budgeted out, so sometimes I would come out about $3-5 richer in one day.

Some of you may be reading this thinking, "Five bucks? That's chump change!" May I remind you that this was the early- to mid-1990s, and I was in elementary school, so an extra three to five bucks went a lot further then. I remember when I was about seven or eight, and I could stretch $1 so far that it wasn't even funny. I could buy a bag of chips, a Little Debbie cake, and a juice all for seventy- five cents. That left me with twenty-five cents to spend on candy, which I could secure for about five cents a pop!

Two things immediately come to mind: first, there's no way I can get anything remotely edible for five cents today. And two, my goodness, my diet was god-awful! I essentially got hopped up on sugar for about a dollar, which probably explained why my parents called me hyperactive all the time.

But to my first point, there's a reason why I can't get anything edible for five cents today; it's because of inflation. **Inflation, in economic terms, refers to the phenomenon where the cost of goods rises while purchasing power (your dollar) falls.** (21)

Looking back on my childhood, we are able to get a sense of how inflation works. Just think about it: I was able to buy a 1.75 oz bag of Doritos for $0.25. That same bag today costs double or triple that price! Many of the same snacks that you could essentially buy for pennies cost dollars today. That's how inflation works. The price of those snacks rose while the strength of your dollar fell. In essence, it costs you more to buy less! A fun and potentially sad game is to ask your parents and grandparents how much different items cost when they were children. Ask them how much a house, car, movie ticket, tuition, a steak dinner, etc. cost when they were your age. Inflation plays an important role in driving the costs of goods and services, and there are plenty of complicated details that experts can't even fully gauge or agree upon. A vital part of our central banking system (The Fed) is controlling inflation, and as we've seen over years, their job is a lot more art than science. Good thing for us, we're not here to explore all the intricacies of The Fed as it relates to inflation. We're not here to fight that fight. We're simply here to get a high-level understanding of what inflation is, and how it looks in our everyday lives.

In basketball, inflation is most often associated with stats. In my opinion, it's a lot easier to understand inflation in basketball terms than in economic terms. We all know inflated stats when we see them, even if the person putting up those stats plays for our home team. You know the kind of player I'm talking about. It's the guy who averages a juicy stat line, yet his team always misses the playoffs. Without taking shots at any current players, let's take a look back at some of the highest scoring teams in NBA history to drive home our concept of inflation. The top three scoring teams in NBA history were the 1981-1982 Denver Nuggets (~126ppg), 1961-1962 Philadelphia Warriors (~125ppg), and the 1966-1967 Philadelphia 76ers (125ppg) (22). On the surface, that's pretty baffling. You would surely expect at least one current team to make the list, especially with the major focus on the three-pointer in today's game. Along the same lines, players today are generally better overall players than in the 1960s. From a physical standpoint, today's players are bigger, faster, and stronger than players in the 1960s. From a technological standpoint, there have been so many advances in travel, health, training, etc. Knowing all of this, why are the top three scoring teams in NBA history made up of guys who played basketball four or five decades ago? The simple answer is the game of basketball was a lot different. The more complicated answer is inflation.

During the 1960s, which is when two of these teams played, the pace of the game was dizzying. Since possession tracking didn't emerge until the 1970s, I'll make an educated guess that the number of possessions in the 1960s was greater than or equal to the number of possessions in the 1970s (around 105 per game). That's a lot of possessions, especially when comparing that to today's stats. Over the past couple of years, there have been an average of about 96 possessions per game. (23) That's nearly 10 less possessions per game versus peak possessions in the 1970s.

Now with that in mind, it's easy to see how with 10 more possessions per game you can score 120+ points per game.

Beyond the sheer volume of possessions, basketball was a lot less efficient in the 1960s and 1970s versus today's game. It follows that players' counting stats (points, rebounds, assists, steals, blocks) soared. If someone shoots and misses, someone has to be there to grab the rebound. If someone turns the ball over without it going out of bounds, someone has to be there to steal it. If there are 105+ possessions per game, someone has to use the majority of them. You get the idea. (One very interesting thing to note is that only one of those teams, the 1966-1967 Philadelphia 76ers, won a title; they had the luxury of rolling out Wilt Chamberlain at center every night at a time when centers were closer to today's small forwards.) It's no surprise then that when speaking about inflated stats in NBA history, two of the most identifiable players in question played in the 1960s and 1970s: Oscar Robertson and Wilt Chamberlain.

Oscar Robertson famously averaged a triple-double during the 1961-1962 season (if you combined the Big O's first five seasons in the NBA, his overall averages equate to a triple-double: 30.3 points, 10.4 rebounds, and 10.6 assists per game). (24) Wilt Chamberlain holds upwards of 70 NBA records, two most notably are averaging 50 points for an entire season, and the other is scoring 100 points in a game without any three-pointers. (25) I don't think any true basketball fan or historian questions whether these two players are great; rather, given the makeup of the league when these guys played, do their stats truly represent their greatness or something else? I think the answer is both. On one hand, there have been thousands of players shuttling through the NBA over the past 50 years, and only a handful have achieved what these two titans of the game have. For Chamberlain, the list is even shorter. Robertson's feat isn't anything to sneeze at either, as it took Russell Westbrook 50+ years to average a triple-double for an entire season. That speaks volumes to Chamberlain and Robertson's greatness. However, these guys' stats are most certainly inflated when we account for the pace of the game, the level of talent they faced, the size of the league, and the overall quality of basketball being played in the 1960s and 1970s. It's the same exact concept when your grandparents say they bought a huge house in the nice part of town for $20,000 in 1960, and when you look up the cost of that very same house today, you realize that it's more than $1,000,000. The key takeaway here is numbers without context mean nothing. Housing prices have increased significantly since the 1960s, and inflation has been a driving force.

In basketball, inflated stats have largely *decreased* due to advances in the game, better players, rule changes, better game planning, etc. Of course, there are still teams and players alike who put up big numbers without any depth; however, by and large, those types of teams and players have declined since the 1960s and 1970s. It is interesting to note though that today's game is borrowing a few major tenants from yesteryear and adding its own twist. Pace has been creeping up yearly, and more teams are firing from long range. But one of the biggest differences today is the focus on efficiency. This means eliminating long, contested two-pointers, focusing on getting to the basket, and emphasizing free throws, to name a few.

In sum, inflation comes in many forms both in our everyday lives and in sports. Inflation can affect the prices of the most basic things we consume like milk and bread, and extend to larger, more complicated things like investments and homes. In basketball, inflation doesn't always come in the form of big stat lines; inflation is influenced by many different factors from the style of game being played to the time period, and then to the players playing the game.

All in all, inflation can be seen as a barometer of the times, whether in basketball or in the real world.

Author's Bio

John F. McMichael was born and raised in Brooklyn, NY. Over the past 10 years, John has worked on Wall Street at some of the most prestigious firms in finance, including Bloomberg L.P, JP Morgan Chase, and Loop Capital Markets. John currently resides in Los Angeles, CA, where he works in Private Wealth Management at Goldman Sachs.

John is a Posse Scholar, who attended Vanderbilt University. He graduated with a bachelor's degree in Global Corporate Finance and Management.

Growing up, John played multiple sports, but his true love was always basketball. From his days traveling across the country playing AAU to more recently coaching middle school basketball, John has spent 20+ years around the game. John decided to write this book because he truly believes in giving back, and what better way to give back than to marry his technical skills with his passion for basketball to provide financial literacy to those who need it the most?

Contact information
Email: jmcmichael06@gmail.com
Instagram: iamjohn.f.mcmichael
Facebook: John McMichael
Twitter: @john_mcmichael1

Sources

1. https://www.investopedia.com/terms/s/scarcity.asp
2. https://www.forbes.com/billionaires/list/4/#version:static
3. https://www.basketball-reference.com/players/w/westbru01.html
4. https://www.investopedia.com/university/economics/economics3.asp
5. https://www.si.com/nba/2016/07/01/mike-conley-memphis-grizzlies-free-agent-contract-signs
6. https://www.investopedia.com/terms/c/cost-benefitanalysis.asp
7. https://www.investopedia.com/terms/l/lawofdiminishingmarginalreturn.asp
8. http://www.businessdictionary.com/definition/tradeoff.html
9. https://www.investopedia.com/terms/o/opportunitycost.asp
10. https://www.investopedia.com/terms/r/risktolerance.asp
11. https://www.investopedia.com/terms/s/stock.asp
12. https://www.investopedia.com/terms/e/equity.asp
13. https://www.investopedia.com/terms/b/bond.asp
14. https://www.investopedia.com/terms/a/assetallocation.asp
15. https://www.investopedia.com/terms/d/diversification.asp
16. http://www.cleveland.com/business/index.ssf/2016/01/why_do_70_percent_of_lottery_w.html
17. https://www.investopedia.com/terms/n/networth.asp
18. https://www.investopedia.com/terms/l/liquidity.asp

19. https://www.investopedia.com/terms/t/timevalue ofmoney.asp
20. https://www.investopedia.com/terms/c/compoun dinterest.asp
21. https://www.investopedia.com/university/inflation/inflation1.asp
22. https://www.basketball-reference.com/leaders/team_pts.html
23. https://www.basketball-reference.com/leagues/NBA_stats.html
24. https://www.basketball-reference.com/players/r/roberos01.html
25. https://www.basketball-reference.com/players/c/chambwi01.html

Intentionally Left Blank

Made in the USA
San Bernardino, CA
27 March 2019